Quotable Quotes Excellence

Vol. 1 of 20
Knowledge & Secrets

CHARLES MWEWA

Copyright © 2023 Charles Mwewa

www.charlesmwewa.com

Published by:

ACP

Ottawa, Ontario

Canada

www.acpress.ca

www.springopus.com

All rights reserved.

ISBN: 978-1-988251-93-6

DEDICATION

For

Charles Chibwe

CONTENTS

DEDICATION	iii
CONTENTS	v
AUTHOR'S WORD	vii
KNOWLEDGE & SECRETS	
Mostly Knowledge	1
Mostly Secrets	49
Knowledge, Secrets and More	77
ABOUT THE AUTHOR	183
SELECTED BOOKS BY THIS AUTHOR	185
INDEX	191

AUTHOR'S WORD

Wisdom is supreme. Wisdom is grand. Wisdom is the ultimate excellence. If you want to get anything, get wisdom. The best way to be wise and to gain wisdom is to observe, and a lot of it.

Life has a pattern; words have the power to change anything. But only words which alliterate sound and meaning and natural reality, have that power – the power to see clearly, to understand complex ideas and to apply them to real life situations, and be better.

The nuggets provided in this book of *Quotable Quotes Excellence, Vol. 1: Knowledge & Secrets* (in a series of 20), are prepared for you – if you love wisdom and thinking.

cm.

KNOWLEDGE & SECRETS

Mostly Knowledge

1. "Seek knowledge even if you have to knock at the very entrance of heaven."

2. "The earth is like a large pizza; you can only get a piece of it to the extent to which you know."

3. "You are defeated based on what you don't know; you succeed because of what you know."

Quotable Action

◄ What I learned from the quotes:

▼ What I will do with what I learned:

4. "The mind is like a large ocean, no matter how many rivers of knowledge flow into it, it never gets filled."

5. "How can a boy born poor and a nobody change his destiny, by the knowledge of what is and what makes."

6. "If you want to make progress from where you are, simply know more than where you are."

Quotable Action

◄ What I learned from the quotes:

▼ What I will do with what I learned:

7. "There is no monopoly of knowledge; you can find it in books, patches, nature and around you."

8. "God wants you to know more about everything, all things."

9. "Only what the brain knows gives rise to what your body does."

Quotable Action

◀ What I learned from the quotes:

▼ What I will do with what I learned:

10. "Learn to know, and you have known the heart that beats in winners."

11. "There is no bigger problem than ignorance; if you don't know, you have a problem."

12. "There is no difference between ignorance and the grave, both kill potential."

Quotable Action

◄ What I learned from the quotes:

▼ What I will do with what I learned:

13. "Know yourself first."

14. "The first knowledge you must pursue is to know what you are good at; then improve on it."

15. "It's better to improve on what you know than wasting time attending to what you don't know."

Quotable Action

◄ What I learned from the quotes:

▼ What I will do with what I learned:

16. "To be a good teacher, you must know what your students know."

17. "To be a good student, you must aim at knowing what your teacher knows, and exceed it."

18. "The only thing that beats worry is knowledge."

Quotable Action

◄ What I learned from the quotes:

▼ What I will do with what I learned:

19. "The only exam that you achieve zero percent in, is the one you did not take."

20. "You can't say you can be anything if you can't read about everything."

21. "Knowledge is like a bright light, wherever it shows up, the darkness of ignorance flees."

Quotable Action

◄ What I learned from the quotes:

▼ What I will do with what I learned:

22.   "The only reason you are where you are is because you don't know anything different."

23.   "The knowledge of only one discipline is a curse; you only think from one perspective, your own."

24.   "You can't think more than you know."

Quotable Action

◀ What I learned from the quotes:

▼ What I will do with what I learned:

25. "You can't be more than you know."

26. "Ideas are brain children of knowledge, the less you know, the less ideas you have."

27. "To the ignorant, a hill is a mountain."

Quotable Action

◀ What I learned from the quotes:

▼ What I will do with what I learned:

28.   "Knowledge of what is, is sorrow, but knowledge of how to, is what brings gold out of an ore."

29.   "The best way to know is to ask questions."

30.   "Even faith is the substance of things *hoped* for; there is knowledge before there is faith."

Quotable Action

◄ What I learned from the quotes:

▼ What I will do with what I learned:

31.   "Faith comes by hearing, without knowledge, there is little chance for salvation."

32.   "It is easier to confuse presumption with knowledge."

33.   "Don't marry the person you don't know - it'll be like building a house from the roof."

Quotable Action

◄ What I learned from the quotes:

▼ What I will do with what I learned:

34. "If what you are doing is not working for you, learn something new; it's never too late to change a profession."

35. "Most people think that they don't love something; but they just don't know it that well."

36. "You will always hate what you don't know very well, this includes your significant others."

Quotable Action

◄ What I learned from the quotes:

▼ What I will do with what I learned:

37. "A fool says in his heart that there is no God; he's a fool because he doesn't know."

38. "Money doesn't make you rich; what makes you rich is the knowledge of how to make, use and keep money."

39. "The only thing that conquers the future is knowledge."

Quotable Action

◄ What I learned from the quotes:

▼ What I will do with what I learned:

40. "You prayed about it, now know about it, and you will have your answer."

41. "The ignorant are the most abused, intimidated and impoverished people on earth."

42. "If the reason why you are where you are is because someone told you there weren't better things elsewhere, they lied to you."

Quotable Action

◄ What I learned from the quotes:

▼ What I will do with what I learned:

43. "The only reason why Africa sells itself to the West is because Africa doesn't know its value."

44. "A small heart has no love; a small mind lacks knowledge."

45. "Knowledge expands you in ways that make you a jack of all trades and master of all."

Quotable Action

◀ What I learned from the quotes:

▼ What I will do with what I learned:

46. "Don't follow a leader who doesn't give you a chance to know more than them."

47. "You can have sex with just about any person, but you can only make love with a person you know."

48. "You can only boast about the thing you know well."

Quotable Action

◄ What I learned from the quotes:

▼ What I will do with what I learned:

49. "To be ruled by an ignorant leader is worse than falling into a ditch, it's falling into hell."

50. "Don't be afraid to fail, to be rejected or to be disappointed, just know how to succeed, accept yourself and appoint yourself."

51. "If you don't know what they are saying, even if they say something good about you, you will not know."

Quotable Action

◄ What I learned from the quotes:

▼ What I will do with what I learned:

52.   "The more languages you know, the faster your brain works; why should UK with only English conquer Africa with so many languages?"

53.   "Ignorance of the law is not a defence, so is ignorance of anything, it leaves you defenceless."

54.   "Knowledgeable people live many more years after their death; ignorant people died years before their death."

Quotable Action

◄ What I learned from the quotes:

▼ What I will do with what I learned:

55. "When you fly in an airplane you begin to wonder how little you know about what surrounds you; you can't exhaust knowledge."

56. "Only those who know their God will do exploits."

57. "Satan envies those who love God, but he is afraid of those who know God."

Quotable Action

◄ What I learned from the quotes:

▼ What I will do with what I learned:

58. "The best time to add to your k-NOW-ledge is NOW."

59. "If you know before you do, you will always be ahead of the competition."

60. "Spying comes before conquest, as knowledge comes before achievement."

Quotable Action

◀ What I learned from the quotes:

▼ What I will do with what I learned:

61. "Ignorance comes from 'ignore' - not because there is nothing to learn."

62. "Age is irrelevant to knowledge; you can pursue your first degree even at 70 years old."

63. "Find time, make time or borrow time, to pursue knowledge."

Quotable Action

◄ What I learned from the quotes:

▼ What I will do with what I learned:

64. "The desire to know was what brought the first sin into the world; knowledge of the truth is what takes away sin from the world."

65. "Preaching/teaching others about the topics you least know or have not experienced, is like leading sheep from behind."

66. "There are people who pretend to know and they don't know; and there are those who know and pretend they don't know."

Quotable Action

◄ What I learned from the quotes:

▼ What I will do with what I learned:

67. "Know your friends well, your enemies better, and yourself completely."

68. "The difference between advertisement and education; the former tells little of what you want, the latter more of what you need."

69. "The difference between knowledge and brainwashing; the latter is listening to the same lies many times till they sound true."

Quotable Action

◄ What I learned from the quotes:

▼ What I will do with what I learned:

70.   "Before you say 'Yes,' know; before you say 'No,' investigate."

71.   "Words said to destroy you can be conquered by knowledge."

Quotable Action

◀ What I learned from the quotes:

▼ What I will do with what I learned:

Mostly Secrets

72.   "There is no revelation without secrets."

73.   "There are certain things about you that only God should know."

74.   "When people know your secrets, you become predictable; predictable people are expendable."

Quotable Action

◄ What I learned from the quotes:

▼ What I will do with what I learned:

75. "Defend your secrets, the future of your destiny depends on them."

76. "Once a secret is known, the only thing that can restore it is war."

77. "A prostitute sells her body for sex; but she who reveals her secrets sells her soul for nothing."

Quotable Action

◄ What I learned from the quotes:

▼ What I will do with what I learned:

78. "Once I know your name, date of birth and telephone number or email address, you may be my slave."

79. "How did Europe conquer Africa, Europe first learned about Africa."

80. "Nations whose secrets are known to everybody are vulnerable, and so are individuals."

Quotable Action

◄ What I learned from the quotes:

▼ What I will do with what I learned:

81. "Some secrets are not meant to be revealed; they are meant to be concealed."

82. "If you can't keep a secret, you can't defend a city."

83. "No number of weapons and defence can save you from destruction, if your enemy knows your secrets."

Quotable Action

◀ What I learned from the quotes:

▼ What I will do with what I learned:

84. "The only reason why you're in trouble is because they discovered your secret; if you keep a secret, no trouble will come."

85. "With secrets, an empire becomes invincible, and businesses are protected."

86. "The first thing your enemy will use to defeat you, is your secret."

Quotable Action

◄ What I learned from the quotes:

▼ What I will do with what I learned:

87. "Only give your secrets to a wise person; they will protect you in the day of calamity."

88. "To whom you reveal all your secrets, from that person's hand you will fall."

89. "Your secret is your last line of defence; if it falls, so does your guard."

Quotable Action

◄ What I learned from the quotes:

▼ What I will do with what I learned:

90. "Secrecy is an 11ᵗʰ commandment."

91. "What is the definition of foolishness? It is revealing what is meant to be a secret, and keeping sealed what is meant to be open."

92. "The secret that God doesn't want to reveal Himself to us physically, is a revelation called faith."

Quotable Action

◄ What I learned from the quotes:

▼ What I will do with what I learned:

93. "Dogs don't eat dogs; so, a wise person doesn't devour secrets."

94. "A leader is the one called to protect secrets."

95. "Your way to victory, progress and prosperity is a secret; if you discover it, it becomes your victory, progress and prosperity."

Quotable Action

◄ What I learned from the quotes:

▼ What I will do with what I learned:

96. "Wars are won by secrets; nations are governed because of secrets."

97. "Secrets are made for wise minds; foolishness is in the words of an open mouth."

98. "Don't tell your partner the truth about their sexual performance, tell them the truth of the future performance you desire."

Quotable Action

◄ What I learned from the quotes:

▼ What I will do with what I learned:

99. "Although we are born naked, God does not want us to live naked."

100. "Truth is a weapon, and so is a secret."

101. "Jesus is truth, and yet He was hidden in Scripture."

102. "Only the truth that you can defend is worth revealing, everything else will lead to misunderstandings."

Quotable Action

◄ What I learned from the quotes:

▼ What I will do with what I learned:

103. "Sometimes, it is plain stupidity to tell someone the truth; if truth is used to destroy, it can destroy, indeed."

104. "Yes, there are some secrets you must hide from your spouse, if you expose them carelessly, you may have murdered love."

105. "A secret is a powerful weapon; nations rise and fall to the extent to which their secrets are exposed."

Quotable Action

◄ What I learned from the quotes:

▼ What I will do with what I learned:

106. "Do you know that God is in everything everywhere, but only those who seek Him will find Him?"

107. "If a women exposes are agents of beauty very easily, she has lost value in the main."

108. "The reason why we hide our genitalia is because secrecy is more valuable than exposure."

Quotable Action

◄ What I learned from the quotes:

▼ What I will do with what I learned:

109. "Jesus used more parables because they hide secrets."

110. "The purpose of a secret is to be revealed; what is achieved by solving a secret, is more valuable than what is direct."

111. "If the secret you hold will only hurt others and doesn't bring any benefit, do not share it with others."

Quotable Action

◄ What I learned from the quotes:

▼ What I will do with what I learned:

112. "In life and leadership, assume things will be difficult, prepare for the impossible and pray for the possible."

113. "Trust keeps secrets."

Quotable Action

◀ What I learned from the quotes:

▼ What I will do with what I learned:

Knowledge, Secrets and More

114. "Ultimately, speculations should lead to opinions, opinions to belief and belief to knowledge; those who know, will be above reproach."

115. "In the end, knowledge will rule."

116. "The ignorant may sustain some victories, and even become successful, but in the end, they come up short."

Quotable Action

◄ What I learned from the quotes:

▼ What I will do with what I learned:

117. "The ignorant and a fool have one thing in common, they are both unwilling to know."

118. "Learning is a process; knowledge is the destination and the means to the same."

119. "Learners become earners."

Quotable Action

◄ What I learned from the quotes:

▼ What I will do with what I learned:

120. "Learning has rewards just like earning does."

121. "Knowledge becomes the atmosphere in which creativity thrives."

122. "Knowledge is the unwrapping of a secret."

123. "The interest on life is shrouded in mystery, only those who discover the secret will enjoy its benefits."

Quotable Action

◀ What I learned from the quotes:

▼ What I will do with what I learned:

124. "Those who know are rarely deceived."

125. "The knowledge of oneself, and of an opponent, are the pathways to finesse."

126. "You cannot discover a secret without knowledge."

127. "A secret revealed opens the gate, but knowledge gives you the legs to walk through."

Quotable Action

◄ What I learned from the quotes:

▼ What I will do with what I learned:

128. "Revelation is the end of all secrets."

129. "There are secrets that need not to be revealed, and there is knowledge that needs not to be acquired."

130. "Good knowledge gives power, bad knowledge disempowers."

Quotable Action

◀ What I learned from the quotes:

▼ What I will do with what I learned:

131. "Good secrets are meant to be revealed, bad secrets are mean to be concealed."

132. "Like a bomb, a secret perishes by its own ingredients."

133. "The secrets of nature are deciphered by the knowledge of the author of life."

Quotable Action

◄ What I learned from the quotes:

▼ What I will do with what I learned:

134. "Life is encoded in secrets, but knowledge is the key that unlocks it."

135. "A teacher is like a pizza delivery driver; she may smell the knowledge but she may not benefit from it."

136. "When a student becomes a teacher, she becomes greater than her former teacher."

Quotable Action

◄ What I learned from the quotes:

▼ What I will do with what I learned:

137. "There is one secret that should always be revealed, a secret that you have a secret."

138. "There is one knowledge that you must always have, the knowledge that you must know."

139. "Every secret will, ultimately, be revealed whether in this life or in the next."

Quotable Action

◄ What I learned from the quotes:

▼ What I will do with what I learned:

140. "Knowledge must not perish with death; publish it and it will keep you alive for eternity."

141. "Everything you know will count in the day of your death."

142. "Judgment assumes that you know, so be ready to account even for what you do not know."

Quotable Action

◄ What I learned from the quotes:

▼ What I will do with what I learned:

143. "Intelligence is the management of what you know and the experimentation in secrets."

144. "Intelligence gathers information with a view to knowledge."

145. "There are secrets that are worth dying for."

Quotable Action

◄ What I learned from the quotes:

▼ What I will do with what I learned:

146. "There is knowledge that is worth living for."

147. "Memory is the storehouse of knowledge and the key to secrets."

148. "Memory, knowledge and secrets do not live far away from rumors."

149. "A rumor is knowledge that has been imprisoned by secrets."

Quotable Action

◄ What I learned from the quotes:

▼ What I will do with what I learned:

150. "Speculation is the bodyguard for knowledge and gossiper of secrets."

151. "Knowledge is a castle, those who know are well defended."

152. "If you keep adding knowledge to knowledge, you will eventually become both free and sorrowful."

Quotable Action

◄ What I learned from the quotes:

▼ What I will do with what I learned:

153. "The more secrets you defend, the more enemies you will have."

154. "Better to know than to be arbiter over secrets."

155. "If you have more secrets than knowledge, you will be in danger of exposure."

Quotable Action

◄ What I learned from the quotes:

▼ What I will do with what I learned:

156. "If you have more knowledge than secrets, you will survive many traps."

157. "If you remember more than you know, you may be delusional."

158. "If you know more than you remember, you may lose simple battles."

Quotable Action

◄ What I learned from the quotes:

▼ What I will do with what I learned:

159. "If you speculate more than you know, you live by chance."

160. "If you know more than you speculate, you will be as strong as a rock."

161. "If you remember more than you speculate, you will win."

Quotable Action

◄ What I learned from the quotes:

▼ What I will do with what I learned:

162. "If you speculate more than you remember, you will lose."

163. "Knowledge is responsive, information is reactive."

164. "You do something to acquire knowledge, but you do something about what you know to inform or be informed."

Quotable Action

◄ What I learned from the quotes:

▼ What I will do with what I learned:

165. "Education and experience give us knowledge; information breaks them even."

166. "You may not be informed without knowing, but you can always be informed when you know; you can't be informed without knowing."

167. "If you can choose what you know, you can control the outcomes."

Quotable Action

◄ What I learned from the quotes:

▼ What I will do with what I learned:

168.   "Information is facts that have been known."

169.   "Unless information becomes knowledge, it may not benefit you that much."

170.   "Many nations are informed, but few nations know."

Quotable Action

◄ What I learned from the quotes:

▼ What I will do with what I learned:

171. "The developed countries have mastered the skill of translating information into knowledge."

172. "If the developing countries can know, they can innovate."

173. "If someone deprives you of both knowledge and information, you become their slave."

Quotable Action

◂ What I learned from the quotes:

▾ What I will do with what I learned:

174. "You can't know for another; you can only have information for another."

175. "Childishness may also be defined as always being informed; maturity comes with knowledge."

176. "Information is useless unless it can be turned into useful knowledge."

Quotable Action

◄ What I learned from the quotes:

▼ What I will do with what I learned:

177. "Anything that adds value to either knowledge or information is news."

178. "News comes from the word 'new' because there is no news unless prior information has been superseded by something newer."

179. "The difference between old information and news is the value that the former lacked."

Quotable Action

◄ What I learned from the quotes:

▼ What I will do with what I learned:

180. "You can always become news when you add value to your knowledge."

181. "News is always a moving target."

182. "Every secret has a lifespan."

Quotable Action

◄ What I learned from the quotes:

▼ What I will do with what I learned:

183. "The rule of secrecy resonates with the corollaries of light, darkness, public and privacy."

184. "Secrets, whether bad or good, end up showing up."

185. "The end of every secret is to be discovered."

Quotable Action

◄ What I learned from the quotes:

▼ What I will do with what I learned:

186. "Wisdom protects another's secrets, but the fool thinks that disclosing another's secrets is great gain."

187. "The goal of a good judge is to see beyond the façade and to expose secrets."

188. "Just behind any secret lies the truth."

Quotable Action

◀ What I learned from the quotes:

▼ What I will do with what I learned:

189. "Wrongs hidden embondage, but the ones disclosed, liberate."

190. "Those who disclose their faults will taste freedom; but those who hide them, will suffer shame."

191. "The glory of searching secrets out, is royalty."

Quotable Action

◄ What I learned from the quotes:

▼ What I will do with what I learned:

192. "To be authentic, the gods must hide the truth for the mortals to search out."

193. "The pride of daylight is forged by the pangs of nighttime."

194. "People's secret sins don't escape the light of God's presence."

Quotable Action

◀ What I learned from the quotes:

▼ What I will do with what I learned:

195. "Anything you don't know about, to you, it could be a secret."

196. "Every great leader finds a few men he can disclose his secrets to."

197. "More often than not, truth does not come standard."

Quotable Action

◀ What I learned from the quotes:

▼ What I will do with what I learned:

198. "True giving is secretive."

199. "Even good news may be received as bad news."

200. "Even bad news may be conceived as good news."

201. "Silence does not befit good news."

Quotable Action

◀ What I learned from the quotes:

▼ What I will do with what I learned:

202. "The purpose of information is the knowledge that it effuses."

203. "News begets response."

204. "Unless knowledge become news, it remains but a pipedream."

Quotable Action

◄ What I learned from the quotes:

▼ What I will do with what I learned:

205. "More often than not, knowledge is not the end in itself."

206. "The news is the medium."

207. "Good news refreshes."

208. "News must be heard to be news."

Quotable Action

◀ What I learned from the quotes:

▼ What I will do with what I learned:

209. "Good news puts fat on the bones" (Proverbs 15:30).

210. "The knowledge of bad news pierces like a dagger."

211. "The ease with which good news is released can only be matched with the wisdom with which bad news must be communicated."

Quotable Action

◄ What I learned from the quotes:

▼ What I will do with what I learned:

212. "There might be more bad news in the way bad news is communicated than in the bad news itself."

213. "There is heart in discharging good news, in bad news, there must be thought."

214. "Speculations, opinions, information, knowledge, yes — even good or bad news, can be weaponized."

Quotable Action

◄ What I learned from the quotes:

▼ What I will do with what I learned:

215. "News is like medicine; you only need it if you are sick."

216. "What is news to one, may be a bother to another."

217. "To those it impacts, news is like a comforting seat."

Quotable Action

◄ What I learned from the quotes:

▼ What I will do with what I learned:

218. "Good news is relative."

219. Bad news is absolute."

220. "Opinions must always be given in good faith, and be taken with a pinch of salt."

Quotable Action

◄ What I learned from the quotes:

▼ What I will do with what I learned:

221. "An opinion should be prefixed with, 'I give my opinion in this matter,' otherwise, stated in no ambiguous terms."

222. "Do not fear to opine; opinions have built empires and destroyed others."

223. "The last thing you do, must be to reveal your mind."

Quotable Action

◄ What I learned from the quotes:

▼ What I will do with what I learned:

224. "A fool does not delight in understanding," (Proverbs 18:2).

225. "Strive to understand and not to be understood, unless your opinion is uncertain."

226. "Prudence is a game of those who play in the arena of wisdom."

Quotable Action

◀ What I learned from the quotes:

▼ What I will do with what I learned:

227. "If you fear to be misunderstood, at best, give an opinion."

228. "Opinions are not authoritative, unless they are opinions of verifiable experts."

229. "You can appear to have nothing and yet you have everything."

Quotable Action

◄ What I learned from the quotes:

▼ What I will do with what I learned:

230. "You can appear to have much, and yet you have very little."

231. "The world is one third false-mongers, one third fake-mongers, and one third truth-seekers."

232. "To dwell long on two opinions, is a sign of indecision."

Quotable Action

◄ What I learned from the quotes:

▼ What I will do with what I learned:

233. "'Come now, and let us reason together,' says the Lord," (Isaiah 1:18).

234. "Do not quarrel over opinions, discuss them."

235. "Try to seek the approval of men, otherwise of God, but not to please men."

236. "Do not pass judgment on another, unless it is your job to judge."

Quotable Action

◄ What I learned from the quotes:

▼ What I will do with what I learned:

237. "Do not despise another, in thought or in deed."

238. "Human judgment is, generally, a matter of opinion rather than of truth."

239. "Let every person be quick to hear, slow to speak, slow to anger," (James 1:19).

Quotable Action

◄ What I learned from the quotes:

▼ What I will do with what I learned:

240. "Before you propose, have an opinion."

241. "One is loved or hated because of another's opinion."

242. "Break a lie, even if it offends an oath or very important persons."

Quotable Action

◄ What I learned from the quotes:

▼ What I will do with what I learned:

243. "The opinion of the people can be a defence or a weapon."

244. "If you don't have the answer to, 'What is truth?' Stop."

245. "People should not judge what they approve, but must question what they doubt."

Quotable Action

◄ What I learned from the quotes:

▼ What I will do with what I learned:

246. "Whatever does not proceed from faith is sin, but what can't be proved can still be truth."

247. "Testing is good discernment."

248. "What you can't conform to, transform."

Quotable Action

◄ What I learned from the quotes:

▼ What I will do with what I learned:

249. "As the train follows its head, so the body a transformed mind."

250. "When an opinion is strong enough to warrant no further debate, it becomes a belief."

251. "The default position in all relationships is seeking for peace."

Quotable Action

◄ What I learned from the quotes:

▼ What I will do with what I learned:

252. "Fear the crowds' opinion, it could pour out venom."

253. "Fearlessness, power, love and self-control govern those who understand empire building."

254. "Belief in the concept of government is divine; but belief in government is human."

Quotable Action

◄ What I learned from the quotes:

▼ What I will do with what I learned:

255. "The knowledge of appointing authority is superior to the activities of the appointed authorities."

256. "The fact of a thing is that which establishes it."

257. "Gossip is lame, because it is based on unconfirmed facts."

Quotable Action

◀ What I learned from the quotes:

▼ What I will do with what I learned:

258. "Gossip is just another name for a false report."

259. "The mouth must allow truth out first, knowledge second, good news third, opinions third, and gossip last or not at all."

260. "Defaming another person is sitting in judgment against your best conscience."

Quotable Action

◄ What I learned from the quotes:

▼ What I will do with what I learned:

261. "Slander puts the victim thereof in danger."

262. "Slander gives away a fool."

263. "Gossip betrays confidence."

264. "Gossip separates close friends."

Quotable Action

◀ What I learned from the quotes:

▼ What I will do with what I learned:

265. "Whoever would foster love covers over an offense, but whoever repeats the matter separates close friends," (Proverbs 17:9).

266. "Gossip invades the soul."

267. "Avoid anyone who talks too much."

Quotable Action

◄ What I learned from the quotes:

▼ What I will do with what I learned:

268. "Gossip inflames quarrels."

269. "Anyone who imagines the worst against you, is your enemy."

Quotable Action

◄ What I learned from the quotes:

▼ What I will do with what I learned:

270. "You must love knowledge the same way you should love understanding."

271. "Secure your secrets with God."

272. "Use what you know to get to what you don't know."

Quotable Action

◄ What I learned from the quotes:

▼ What I will do with what I learned:

273. "If your secrets don't profit you at all, disclose them."

274. "Let not people's negative opinion of you become your reality."

275. "Broadcast what you know about who you know you are."

Quotable Action

◄ What I learned from the quotes:

▼ What I will do with what I learned:

276. "Sad is an epitaph that should read, 'Here lies a person who did not want to know but was full of secrets.'"

277. "Only when a disease is well diagnosed can be effectively treated."

278. "Leaders must be readers, because they must know."

Quotable Action

◄ What I learned from the quotes:

▼ What I will do with what I learned:

ABOUT THE AUTHOR

Best Selling Author, Charles Mwewa (LLB; BA Law; BA Ed; LLM), is a prolific researcher, poet, novelist, lawyer, law professor and Christian apologist and intercessor. Mwewa has written no less than 80 books and counting in every genre and has exhibited his works at prestigious expos like the Ottawa International Book Expo and is the winner of the Coppa Awards for his signature publication, *Zambia: Struggles of My People*.

SELECTED BOOKS BY THIS AUTHOR

1. *ZAMBIA: Struggles of My People (First and Second Editions)*
2. *10 FINANCIAL & WEALTH ATTITUDES TO AVOID*
3. *10 STRATEGIES TO DEFEAT STRESS AND DEPRESSION: Creating an Internal Safeguard against Stress and Depression*
4. *100+ REASONS TO READ BOOKS*
5. *A CASE FOR AFRICA?S LIBERTY: The Synergistic Transformation of Africa and the West into First-World Partnerships*
6. *A PANDEMIC POETRY, COVID-19*
7. *ALLERGIC TO CORRUPTION: The Legacy of President Michael Sata of Zambia*
8. *BOOK ABOUT SOMETHING: On Ultimate Purpose*
9. *CAMPAIGN FOR AFRICA: A Provocative Crusade for the Economic and Humanitarian Decolonization of Africa*
10. *CHAMPIONS: Application of Common Sense and Biblical Motifs to Succeed in Both Worlds*
11. *CORONAVIRUS PRAYERS*
12. *HH IS THE RIGHT MAN FOR ZAMBIA: And Other Acclaimed Articles on Zambia and Africa*
13. *I BOW: 3500 Prayer Lines of Inspiration & Intercession from the Heart: Volume One*
14. *INTERUNIVERSALISM IN A NUTSHELL: For Iranian Refugee Claimants*
15. *LAW & GRACE: An Expository Study in the Rudiments of Sin and Truth*
16. *LAWS OF INFLUENCE: 7even Lessons in Transformational Leadership*
17. *LOVE IDEAS IN COVID PANDEMIC TIMES:*

For Couples & Lovers
18. *P.A.S.S: Version 2: Answer Bank*
19. *P.A.S.S.: Acing the Ontario Paralegal-Licensing Examination, Version 2*
20. *POETRY: The Best of Charles Mwewa*
21. *QUOT-EBOS: Essential. Barbs. Opinions. Sayings*
22. *REASONING WITH GOD IN PRAYER: Poetic Verses for Peace & Unconfronted Controversies*
23. *RESURRECTION: (A Spy in Hell Novel)*
24. *I DREAM OF AFRICA: Poetry of Post-Independence Africa, the Case of Zambia*
25. *SERMONS: Application of Legal Principles and Procedures in the Life and Ministry of Christ*
26. *SONG OF AN ALIEN: Over 130 Poems of Love, Romance, Passion, Politics, and Life in its Complexity*
27. *TEMPORARY RESIDENCE APPLICATION*
28. *THE GRACE DEVOTIONAL: Fifty-two Happy Weeks with God*
29. *THE SYSTEM: How Society Defines & Confines Us: A Worksheet*
30. *FAIRER THAN GRACE: My Deepest for His Highest*
31. *WEALTH THINKING: And the Concept of Capisolism*
32. *PRAYER: All Prayer Makes All Things Possible*
33. *PRAYER: All Prayer Makes All Things Possible, Answers*
34. *PRISONER OF GRACE: An I Saw Jesus at Milton Vision*
35. *PRAYERS OF OUR CHILDREN*
36. *TEN BASIC LESSONS IN PRAYER*
37. *VALLEY OF ROSES: City Called Beautiful*
38. *THE PATCH THEOREM: A Philosophy of Death, Life and Time*
39. *50 RULES OF POLITICS: A Rule Guide on Politics*
40. *ALLERGIC TO CORRUPTION: The Legacy of*

President Michael Sata of Zambia
41. *INTRODUCTION TO ZAMBIAN ENVIRONMENTAL LEGISLATIVE SCHEME*
42. *REFUGEE PROTECTION IN CANADA: For Iranian Christian Convert Claimants*
43. *LAW & POVERTY (unpublished manuscript)*
44. *CHRISTIAN CONTROVERSIES: Loving Homosexuals*
45. *THINKING GOVERNMENT: Principles & Predilections*
46. *WHY MARRIED COUPLES LIE TO EACH OTHER: A Treatise*
47. *LOVE & FRIENDSHIP TIPS FOR GEN Z*
48. *POVERTY DISCOURSE: Spiritual Imperative or Social Construct*
49. *SEX BEFORE WEDDING: The Tricky Trilemma*
50. *QUOTABLE QUOTES EXCELLENCE, VOL. 1: Knowledge & Secrets*
51. *QUOTABLE QUOTES EXCELLENCE, VOL. 2: Love & Relationships*
52. *QUOTABLE QUOTES EXCELLENCE, VOL. 3: Hope*
53. *QUOTABLE QUOTES EXCELLENCE, VOL. 4: Justice, Law & Morality*
54. *QUOTABLE QUOTES EXCELLENCE, VOL. 5: Dreams & Vision*
55. *QUOTABLE QUOTES EXCELLENCE, VOL. 6: Character & Perseverance*
56. *QUOTABLE QUOTES EXCELLENCE, VOL. 7: Actions*
57. *QUOTABLE QUOTES EXCELLENCE, 1 of 20: Knowledge & Secrets*
58. *QUOTABLE QUOTES EXCELLENCE, 2 of 20: Love & Relationships*
59. *QUOTABLE QUOTES EXCELLENCE, 3 of 20: Hope*

60. *QUOTABLE QUOTES EXCELLENCE, 4 of 20: Justice, Law & Morality*
61. *QUOTABLE QUOTES EXCELLENCE, 5 of 20: Vision & Dreams*
62. *THE SEVEN LAWS OF LOVE*
63. *THE BURDEN OF ZAMBIA*
64. *ETHICAL MENTORSHIP: Missing Link in Transformational Leadership*
65. *AFRICA MUST BE DEVELOPED: Agenda for the 22nd Century Domination*
66. *INNOVATION: The Art of Starting Something New*
67. *TOWARDS TRUE ACHIEVEMENT: The Mundane & the Authentic*
68. *ONE WORLD UNDER PRAYER: For Cameroon, Ecuador and France*
69. *ONE WORLD UNDER PRAYER: For New Zealand, Poland and Uganda*
70. *ONE WORLD UNDER PRAYER: For Malta, USA, and Zambia*
71. *ONE WORLD UNDER PRAYER: For Germany*
72. *ONE WORLD UNDER PRAYER: For Haiti, Iraq, and Russia*
73. *ONE WORLD UNDER PRAYER: For Chad, UN and Syria*
74. *ONE WORLD UNDER PRAYER: For Burundi, Canada, and Israel*
75. *ONE WORLD UNDER PRAYER: For China, Egypt, and Venezuela*
76. *ONE WORLD UNDER PRAYER: For Greece, Mali and Ukraine*
77. *ONE WORLD UNDER PRAYER: For Morocco, North Korea and the UK*
78. *ONE WORLD UNDER PRAYER: For Belgium, Brazil and the Burkina Faso*

QQE: KNOWLEDGE & SECRETS

79. *ADIEU PERFECTIONS: A Satire*
80. *OPTIMIZATION: Turning Low Moments into High Comments*
81. *ACING THE IMPOSSIBLE: Faith in the Other Dimension*
82. *END GAME LAW: Financial Mindset in Quotables*

INDEX

A

advertisement, 45
Africa, 29, 185, 186
agents of beauty, 71
airplane, 37
ambiguous terms, 145
answer, 27
appear, 151
author of life, 87
authorities, 167
authority, 167

B

bad knowledge, 85
bad news, 139
Bad news is absolute, 143
battles, 103
belief, 163
benefits, 81
birth, 53
boast, 31
bodyguard, 99
bomb, 87
bones. *See* fat
books, 5
borrow, 41
brain, 5
brainwashing, 45
bright light, 13
broadcast, 179
by chance, 105

C

calamity, 59
childishness, 115
children, 17
Christian, 183
city, 55
comforting seat, 141
commandment, 61
competition, 39
confidence, 171
conform, 161
conscience, 169
control the outcomes, 109
creativity, 81
crowds, 165
curse, 15

D

dagger, 137
danger of exposure, 101
darkness, 13
death, 35
debate, 163

defeated, 1
defence. *See* law
defenceless. *See* law
degree, 41
delusional, 103
despise, 155
destination, 79
destiny, 51
destroy, 47
developed countries, 113
developing countries, 113
diagnosed. *See* disease
different, 15
discernment, 161
discipline. *See* curse
disease, 181
dogs, 63
doubt, 159
driver, 89

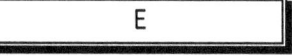

earners, 79
earth, 27
education. *See* advertisement
email, 53
embondage, 125
empire, 57
empire building, 165
empires, 145
enemies, 101
enemy, 55
epitaph, 181
Europe, 53
experience, 109
experimentation, 95
experts, 149

fact, 167
fail, 33
faith, 19
fake-mongers. *See* false-mongers
false-mongers, 151
fat, 137
fear, 149
fearlessness, 165
fool, 25
foolishness, 61
free, 99
freedom, 125
friends, 171
future, 25

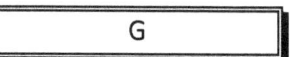

genitalia, 71
God, 37, 186
God's presence, 127
gold, 19
Good news is relative, 143
Good news refreshes, 135
good secrets, 87
gossip, 169
gossiper, 99
government, 165
grave. *See* potential

H

hate, 23
hearing, 21
heart, 29, *See* thought
heaven, 1
hell, 33
house, 21

I

ignorance, 7
improve, 9
in good faith, 143
indecision, 151
information, 95
ingredients. *See* bomb
intelligence, 95
investigate, 47

J

Jesus. *See* truth
judge, 123
judgment, 93, 155

L

languages, 35
law, 35, 183
lawyer, 183
leader, 31, 63
leadership, 75
learn, 23
lifespan, 119

lose, 107
love, 69

M

marry, 21
master, 29
medicine, 141
medium, 135
memory, 97
mind, 3
misunderstandings, 67
money, 25
monopoly, 5
mortals, 127
mountain, 17
mystery, 81

N

naked, 67
nations, 69
negative opinion, 179
news, 117
No. *See* investigate

O

offense, 173
opinions, 77
opponent, 83
ore. *See* gold

P

parables, 73
peace, 163
perspective. *See* curse
pinch of salt, 143
pipedream, 133
pizza, 1
please men, 153
potential, 7
power. *See* fearlessness
pray, 75
preaching. *See* teaching
predictable, 49
presumption, 21
pride, 127
problem, 7
profession. *See* learn
professor, 183
profit, 179
progress, 3
prosperity, 63
prostitute, 51
prudence, 147
public and private, 121
publish, 93

Q

quarrel, 153

R

reactive. *See* responsive
readers, 181
reality, 179
reason together, 153
responsive, 107
revelation, 49
rewards, 81
rich. *See* money
rock, 105
roof. *See* house
royalty, 125
rule of secrecy, 121
rumors, 97

S

salvation, 21
Satan. *See* God
Scripture. *See* Jesus
self-control. *See* fearlessness
sex, 31
sexual performance, 65
shame, 125
sheep, 43
sick. *See* medicine
sin, 161
slander, 171
slave, 53
slow, 155
sorrow, 19
soul, 51
speculations, 77
standard, 129
Struggles of My People, 183, 185
student, 89
students. *See* teacher
stupidity, 69
substance, 19

succeed. *See* fail

T

teacher, 11
teaching, 43
telephone, 53
the West, 29, 185
thought, 139
train, 163
transform. *See* conform
traps, 103
trouble, 57
truth, 67
truth-seekers. *See* false-mongers

U

UK. *See* languages
understanding, 147

V

venom, 165

very important persons, 157
victim, 171
victory, 63

W

war, 51
weapon, 67
weaponized, 139
What is truth?, 159
win, 105
winners, 7
wisdom, 137
world, 43
worry, 11

Y

Yes. *See* investigate
yourself, 9

Z

Zambia, 183, 185, 186, 187
zero percent, 13